Dear Self, I'm Sorry!

jalyn jace

Published by jalyn jace, 2023.

DEAR SELF, I'M SORRY!

First edition. October 29, 2023.

Copyright © 2023 jalyn jace.

ISBN: 979-8223120773

Written by jalyn jace.

Table of Contents

"Don't be afraid to start over. It's a new chance to rebuild your life the way you want it to be."

Dear self,

I'm sorry for not loving myself as much as I should have. I know I'm worthy of love and respect, and I vow to start treating myself with the kindness and care I deserve. I'm ready to start a journey of self-love and acceptance.

Sincerely, Me

The shadows of my past,
Linger in my present,
But I'm determined to make them fast
And learn the lessons they represent.
My flaws are part of me,
And so are my strengths,
I'm learning to love myself,
In all my complexity.
My darkness and my light,
Are no longer in conflict,
I'm taking this journey,
With self-love as its objective.
The shadows of my past,
Are now my greatest ally,
I'm learning to heal them,
And let go of my woes, so readily.
As I continue to grow,
I find self-love and acceptance,
I'm in control of my own fate,
This is the path to my ascension.

Recognizing the Value Within

Each and every one of us is important, possessing inherent value and a unique contribution to make in the world. Our existence matters, and the impact we have on others and the world around us is significant. Embracing our importance is not about seeking validation from external sources, but rather recognizing and honoring the worth and potential that resides within us.

Our importance lies in the connections we forge and the relationships we nurture. The love, support, and understanding we offer to others can have a profound impact on their lives. Our words, actions, and presence can bring comfort, inspiration, and joy to those around us. By recognizing the importance of our relationships, we can cultivate meaningful connections and create a positive ripple effect in the lives of others.

Furthermore, our importance extends to the unique talents, skills, and perspectives we bring to the table. Each of us possesses a set of abilities and experiences that no one else can replicate. By embracing and honing these gifts, we can make a valuable contribution to our communities, workplaces, and society as a whole. Our ideas, creativity, and expertise have the power to bring about positive change and innovation.

Importance also lies in the impact we have on ourselves. By recognizing our own worth and value, we can cultivate self-love, self-care, and personal growth. Taking care of our physical, mental, and emotional well-being allows us to show up fully in our lives and pursue our passions and dreams. When we prioritize our own importance, we become better equipped to make a difference in the lives of others.

It is important to note that our significance is not measured by external achievements or comparisons to others. Each person's journey is unique, and our worth is not determined by societal standards or expectations. Embracing our importance means recognizing that we are enough just as we are, with our own set of strengths, weaknesses, and experiences.

In conclusion, each of us is important, possessing inherent value and a unique contribution to make in the world. Our relationships, talents, and personal growth all play a role in shaping our importance. By recognizing and embracing our worth, we can cultivate meaningful connections, make a positive impact, and lead fulfilling lives. Let us celebrate our importance and the importance of others, knowing that our presence and contributions truly matter.

Mental Health

Mental health encompasses various aspects such as patience, self-love, healing, shadow work, finding peace, setting boundaries, forgiveness, understanding, and awareness. It requires being patient with oneself and allowing time for growth and recovery. Self-love involves nurturing and caring for oneself, prioritizing mental well-being. Healing is a process of addressing past traumas and working towards emotional well-being. Shadow work involves exploring and integrating the hidden or suppressed aspects of oneself. Finding peace involves seeking inner calm and tranquility amidst life's challenges. Setting boundaries is crucial for protecting one's mental health and establishing healthy relationships. Forgiveness involves letting go of resentment and embracing understanding and compassion. Developing awareness helps in recognizing and addressing mental health issues, promoting overall well-being.

Overcoming Mental Health

Mental health is a vital aspect of our overall well-being, yet it is often overlooked or stigmatized in society. Overcoming mental health challenges requires courage, resilience, and a commitment to self-care.

The first step in overcoming mental health challenges is acknowledging the need for help. It takes strength to reach out to professionals such as therapists, counselors, or psychiatrists who can provide guidance and support. Seeking help allows individuals to gain insight into their struggles, understand the root causes, and develop effective strategies for recovery.

Self-reflection is a powerful tool in overcoming mental health issues. It involves examining one's thoughts, emotions, and behaviors to identify patterns and triggers. By cultivating self-awareness, individuals can better understand their mental health challenges and make informed decisions about their well-being. This process may involve journaling, meditation, or engaging in activities that promote self-discovery.

Overcoming mental health challenges often requires developing healthy coping mechanisms. These mechanisms can vary from person to person, but they generally involve engaging in activities that promote relaxation, stress reduction, and emotional well-being. Examples include exercise, practicing mindfulness, engaging in creative outlets, or connecting with supportive communities. By adopting healthy coping mechanisms, individuals can effectively manage their mental health and build resilience.

Having a strong support network is crucial in overcoming mental health challenges. Friends, family, or support groups can provide a safe space for individuals to express their feelings, receive encouragement, and gain perspective. Sharing experiences with others who have faced similar struggles can foster a sense of belonging and reduce feelings of isolation. Building a support network ensures that individuals have a reliable source of emotional support during their journey to recovery.

Overcoming mental challenges often involves making lifestyle changes and prioritizing self-care. This includes adopting healthy habits such as maintaining a balanced diet, getting enough sleep, and engaging in regular physical activity. Additionally, individuals may need to set boundaries, learn to say no, and prioritize activities that bring them joy and fulfillment. By prioritizing self-care, individuals can nurture their mental well-being and create a foundation for long-term recovery.

Mental health challenges are a journey that requires patience, resilience, and self-compassion. By seeking help, engaging in self-reflection, developing healthy coping mechanisms, building a support network, and prioritizing self-care, individuals can gradually overcome their mental health issues and achieve a state of wellness. It is important to remember that everyone's journey is unique, and progress may come in small steps. With determination and support, individuals can reclaim their mental well-being and lead fulfilling lives.

Mental Illness From Youth To AdultHood

Mental illness is a pervasive issue that affects individuals across all age groups. However, when it strikes during one's formative years and remains unaddressed until young adulthood, the consequences can be profound.

Growing up with mental illness often entails a heavy burden of silence. Young individuals may struggle to articulate their emotions, fearing judgment or misunderstanding from their peers and family. This silence can exacerbate their condition, leading to feelings of isolation and despair. For instance, a child with anxiety may find it challenging to express their fears, leading to increased anxiety and avoidance behaviors.

Without timely intervention, mental health issues can escalate, impacting various aspects of an individual's life. Academic performance, social relationships, and overall well-being may suffer as a result. For example, a teenager with undiagnosed depression may experience a decline in grades, withdrawal from social activities, and strained relationships with friends and family.

Seeking help is a crucial step towards recovery and personal growth. When individuals finally reach out for support, they open themselves up to a world of possibilities. Professional guidance, therapy, and medication can provide the tools necessary to manage mental illness effectively. For instance, therapy sessions can help individuals develop coping mechanisms, improve self-esteem, and foster healthier relationships.

Obtaining help during young adulthood allows individuals to embark on a journey of self-discovery. Through therapy and self-reflection, they can gain a deeper understanding of their mental health condition and its impact on their lives. This newfound awareness empowers them to take control of their well-being, make informed decisions, and pursue a fulfilling life.

Dealing with mental illness since a young age and not seeking help until young adulthood can be an arduous journey. The burden of silence, missed opportunities for early intervention, and the subsequent impact on various aspects of life can be overwhelming. However, by recognizing the importance of seeking help and embracing the transformative power of intervention, individuals can embark on a path of self-discovery and growth. It is crucial to break the silence, reach out for support, and embrace the possibilities that lie ahead. With the right resources and a supportive network, individuals can overcome the shadows of mental illness and lead fulfilling lives.

Testimony

Throughout my life, I have been intimately acquainted with the challenges of living with mental illness. From a young age, I grappled with the complexities of my mind, navigating a world that often felt overwhelming and isolating. Marked by resilience, self-discovery, and the unwavering determination to find healing.

As a child, I struggled to understand why my thoughts and emotions seemed to differ from those around me. Anxiety and depression became constant companions, casting a shadow over my formative years. Simple tasks felt insurmountable, and social interactions became a source of immense stress. I felt like an outsider, unable to fully connect with my peers.

Unfortunately, My parents didn't have much knowledge about mental health. They believed that my struggles were just a phase and would eventually pass. As a result, my mental health concerns were overlooked, and I was left to navigate my emotions on my own.

Throughout my childhood and teenage years, My mental health continued to deteriorate. Finding it challenging to concentrate in school, trouble making friends, and often feeling isolated. New challenges emerged. The hormonal changes and societal pressures intensified my struggles with anxiety and depression. I felt overwhelmed by the weight of expectations, both internal and external. I would spend countless nights lying awake, consumed by those anxious thoughts.

As I entered young adulthood, my mental health issues became even more pronounced. I found it increasingly difficult to cope with the demands of daily life. Simple tasks felt overwhelming, and my relationships suffered as a result. I knew deep down that I needed help, but I didn't know where to turn.

Each day presented a new challenge as I navigated the intricacies of my mind while trying to maintain a semblance of normalcy in my everyday life. However, I didn't fully understand what I was going through or how to seek help. The struggles soon began to intensify, leading to a severe mental breakdown. Overwhelmed by anxiety, depression, and a sense of hopelessness, I found myself in a dark place. The weight of my emotions became unbearable, and I contemplated ending my pain through a tragic decision.. overdosing on medication.

My journey of overcoming a mental breakdown and overdosing was a testament to the power of resilience, support, and self-discovery. It was a reminder that even in the darkest moments, there is hope.

In my pursuit of healing, I also educated myself about mental health. I devoured books, articles, and documentaries, seeking to understand the intricacies of the mind and the various treatment options available. This knowledge empowered me to advocate for myself and make informed decisions about my mental health care.

As time went on, I began to notice small but significant changes. I've learned to recognize my triggers and implement healthy coping mechanisms. I discovered the power of self-care, engaging in activities that brought me joy and peace. I've learned to embrace my vulnerabilities and accept that it was okay to ask for help. Through therapy, self-reflection, and the support of my loved ones. Also embracing mindfulness practices, learning to be present in the moment and cultivate self-compassion. I began to rebuild my life with a newfound strength.

The road to recovery was not easy. I've faced numerous obstacles, including therapy sessions that forced myself to confront painful memories and emotions. I encountered setbacks and moments of doubt. However, I refused to let them define me. I understood that healing was not linear and that setbacks were an opportunity for growth. With each setback, I've learned valuable lessons about myself and my resilience deepened.

Therapy sessions became a safe space. To explore my emotions, confront past traumas, and develop healthy coping mechanisms. I've learned to identify triggers and implement strategies to manage my anxiety and depression. It was a process of self-reflection and self-compassion, as I began to understand that my mental health challenges did not define my worth.

Navigating everyday life with mental health challenges was not without its hurdles. I've faced moments of overwhelm, panic attacks, and setbacks. But I learned to be kind to myself, acknowledging that healing was not linear. I celebrate small victories, such as completing a challenging task or facing a fear head-on. These victories became stepping stones towards my overall well-being.

My mental health journey became a part of my identity, but not my entire identity. I embraced my experiences and used them as a source of strength and empathy. I've become an advocate for mental health, sharing my story to break the stigma and raise awareness. I've encouraged open conversations about mental health, reminding others that it is okay to not be okay and that seeking help is a sign of strength.

My story is a reminder that seeking help for mental health issues is crucial, no matter how long the struggle has been. It's never too late to reach out, to find support, and to start the healing process. With the right resources and a supportive network, it is possible to find hope, regain control, and create a brighter future

Today, I continue to navigate the complexities of living with mental illness. It is an ongoing journey, marked by both triumphs and setbacks. But I have learned to embrace my experiences as a part of my identity, rather than allowing them to define me. I am resilient, compassionate, and determined to break the stigma surrounding mental health.

My story is a testament to the strength of the human spirit and the power of self-discovery. It is a reminder that even in the darkest moments, there is hope. I share my journey with the hope that it will inspire others facing similar battles to seek help, embrace self-care, and never give up on their pursuit of healing. Together, we can create a world where mental health is understood, accepted, and supported.

Self Love

The journey of self-love is an important one for us all. It can be a difficult journey, but ultimately, it can lead to a happier and more fulfilling life. Self-love involves learning to accept yourself for who you are, understanding your strengths and weaknesses, and understanding that you are worthy of love and respect. It involves forgiving yourself for the mistakes you have made, setting healthy boundaries, and investing in your relationships. You can start your self-love journey by taking a few moments each day to practice self-care and gratitude. Remember to be kind to yourself and to celebrate the progress you make on your journey!

Definitely an Incredibly powerful and rewarding experience. It is a journey of self-discovery and growth that allows us to better understand ourselves and our own needs. Self love requires us to be honest and vulnerable with ourselves, to take a moment to pause and reflect on how we feel. It also requires us to be kind and forgiving to ourselves, to acknowledge our mistakes and shortcomings without judgment. With a strong foundation of self love, we can better navigate the world around us, build meaningful relationships, and live a happier and more fulfilling life.

Self love can also be a difficult journey, but it is one worth taking. It involves understanding yourself, understanding your strengths and weaknesses, and learning to accept and value yourself as you are. Learning to love and appreciate yourself, despite what others may think of you. It requires taking time to reflect on yourself and your own goals, and learning to forgive yourself for past mistakes. Self love can be challenging, but it is an incredibly rewarding journey that can bring joy and peace to your life.

It is a journey of learning to accept and appreciate yourself for who you are, and to recognize and honor your worth and value. It involves learning to love yourself unconditionally, and to be kind and compassionate to yourself. It is a journey of healing and transformation, of facing your fears and releasing self-limiting beliefs. It is a journey of cultivating self-awareness, self-respect, and self-compassion, and of creating a life that is authentic and fulfilling.

A process of learning to accept, respect, and love ourselves. It involves exploring our innermost thoughts and feelings, understanding our needs and boundaries, and learning to be our own biggest advocate. As we move through the self love journey, we recognize our worth and discover that we are capable of creating a compassionate and supportive relationship with ourselves. This process can be challenging at times, but ultimately leads to greater clarity, confidence, and self-esteem. It is an ongoing process that requires patience, commitment, and self-compassion to help us stay on the path to self-love

Centering Yourself

Centering yourself is an important practice for mental and emotional wellbeing. It involves taking the time to connect with yourself and your innermost thoughts and feelings. This can be done through a variety of activities such as meditation, journaling, yoga, and mindfulness. It helps bring clarity to any difficult feelings you may be experiencing, and can help you to make decisions from a place of inner wisdom and understanding. Centering yourself is an important tool to have in your toolbox for self-care and emotional regulation.

Healing Yourself

Healing yourself is an important part of taking care of your mental, physical, and emotional health. It can involve anything from getting regular exercise to engaging in mindful activities like meditation, journaling, or practicing yoga. Taking time to nourish your mind, body, and soul can help build your resilience to stress and improve your overall well being. Developing a healing routine that works for you is an important step in creating a happier and healthier self. Healing oneself is a profound and transformative journey of self-discovery and self-care. It is a process that involves acknowledging and understanding our wounds, both physical and emotional, and actively working towards their resolution and restoration. Healing oneself requires having the courage to confront our pain, to sit with it, and to allow ourselves to feel and process it fully. It involves taking the time to nurture and prioritize our physical, mental, and spiritual well-being. Healing oneself also involves letting go of past traumas and negative patterns, and embracing self-compassion, forgiveness, and self-love. It is a continuous journey of growth, resilience, and self-empowerment, where we take responsibility for our own healing and become the architects of our own happiness and well-being.

Boundaries

Setting boundaries is an essential aspect of self-care and maintaining healthy relationships. Boundaries serve as guidelines that define our limits, needs, and expectations in various aspects of our lives. They help protect our physical, emotional, and mental well-being. Setting boundaries starts with self-awareness and understanding our own needs and limits. It involves clearly communicating our boundaries to others, which can be done assertively and respectfully. This may involve saying "no" when we feel overwhelmed, expressing our discomfort when someone crosses a boundary, or setting limits on the time and energy we invest in certain relationships or activities. It is important to remember that setting boundaries is not selfish but rather an act of self-respect and self-preservation. By setting and enforcing boundaries, we create a healthier and more balanced environment for ourselves and those around us.

Identifying Triggers

Identifying triggers is a crucial step in understanding and managing our emotional responses. Triggers can be anything that elicits a strong emotional reaction or brings back memories of past traumatic events or distressing experiences. They can be specific situations, people, places, smells, sounds, or even certain thoughts or beliefs. To identify triggers, it is important to pay attention to our emotional reactions and patterns. Keeping a journal or diary can be helpful in recognizing recurring triggers and documenting the thoughts and emotions associated with them. Reflecting on past experiences and their impact on our emotional state can also provide valuable insights. Additionally, seeking feedback from trusted friends, family, or professionals can offer an external perspective and help identify triggers that may not be immediately apparent. By becoming more aware of our triggers, we can take proactive steps to manage and minimize their impact on our well-being.

Childhood Trauma

Dealing with childhood trauma can be a complex and challenging journey, but it is a crucial step towards healing and personal growth. It is important to acknowledge and validate the pain and emotions associated with the traumatic experiences. Seeking professional help from therapists, counselors, or support groups can provide a safe space to explore and process these emotions. Engaging in self-care practices such as mindfulness, meditation, or creative outlets can also be helpful in managing the effects of trauma. Building a strong support system of trusted friends and family members who can provide understanding and empathy is essential. It is important to remember that healing is a gradual process, and it may require patience and perseverance. With time and the right resources, it is possible to overcome childhood trauma and lead a fulfilling and resilient life.

Forgiveness

Forgiving people who have hurt you can be difficult, but it is an essential part of moving on and healing. It is important to remember that forgiveness is not necessarily about condoning the behavior, but rather about releasing negative emotions and allowing yourself to move on. By forgiving those who have hurt you, you can free yourself from the burden of resentment and anger, and reclaim your power. Forgiving can also be an act of self-care, allowing you to focus on your own wellbeing and future. Ultimately, forgiving those who have wronged you can help you to create a more peaceful and positive mindset, and help you to move forward in life.

Forgiveness is profoundly an important concept in life. It is an act of mercy and compassion that allows individuals to move past hurt and resentment and start anew. It is understanding that mistakes were made and accepting that we all are human and prone to error. Forgiveness helps us to heal, letting go of anger and bitterness and finding a way to reconcile with those who have wronged us. It is a way of releasing ourselves from the hurt and allowing us to make peace with our past. In this way, forgiveness can be a powerful tool for personal growth and can serve to strengthen relationships.

Also, serving as an important concept in many cultures and religions. It is a way of letting go of hurt and anger, and of accepting that mistakes have been made. By forgiving, we are able to move forward and build healthier, more meaningful relationships with those we love. Forgiveness is a difficult process, but it can also be incredibly liberating. It allows us to free ourselves from the pain and suffering of past experiences, and to focus on creating more positive, fulfilling relationships.

Forgiveness is an essential part of life and an important part of relationships. It is the act of letting go of resentment and bitterness towards another person. When we forgive, we are able to move on and have healthier relationships based on understanding and compassion. Forgiveness is not about condoning bad behavior, but instead about allowing ourselves to heal and move forward. It is important to remember that forgiveness does not mean forgetting, but rather the ability to accept what has happened and understand that mistakes can be made. Forgiveness allows us to find peace and joy in our lives and helps us to build strong relationships.

Forgiveness is an important emotion to possess in life. It is the ability to let go of pain and hurt and to accept that sometimes things do not always go as planned. Forgiveness is a sign of strength and resilience, as it requires a person to be able to move on from past wrongdoings and accept that life is full of ups and downs. It can help us to free ourselves from our own negative emotions, and it can help us to live a more balanced and fulfilling life. Forgiveness is an essential emotion to cultivate, and it can bring us peace and joy in our lives.

Lastly, Forgiveness is an important part of life, and it is a powerful tool that can help us to heal, learn, and grow. It is a way to let go of pain and hurt, and to move forward in a positive way. It is not easy to forgive, but it is important to remember that it can help to reduce anger and improve relationships. Forgiveness can empower us to move on from difficult moments and become better versions of ourselves. It is a powerful way to start a new chapter in life and to build stronger relationships with those around us.

Patience

Patience is an important life skill that can be used in almost every aspect of life. It involves being able to tolerate difficult and frustrating situations without becoming angry or overwhelmed. Practicing patience can help us to be less reactive and more understanding, and to stay calm in the face of adversity. Patience can also help us to appreciate the little things in life, and to enjoy the journey rather than being focused solely on the destination. With patience, we can better manage our emotions and relationships, and become more productive and successful in our endeavors.

Learning patience can be difficult, but it is a valuable asset that everyone should strive for. It involves understanding and accepting that not everything will go according to plan, and that some things take time. It is important to recognize when it is necessary to be patient, and to try and maintain a sense of calm when faced with difficult situations. Patience can help to reduce stress levels and enable us to better handle challenging situations. With practice and effort, patience can be developed and fostered over time.

Also, serving as a valuable skill that can help us in many aspects of our lives. It can help us to better manage difficult situations, to handle stress more effectively, and to be more understanding of others. Patience can also help us to be more mindful and to be able to take a step back and observe our own thoughts and feelings rather than reacting impulsively. By taking the time to practice patience, we can learn how to be more tolerant, compassionate, and understanding of ourselves and others.

Learning patience is a valuable life skill that can help bring greater peace and contentment to our lives. It can be difficult to practice patience in the midst of chaotic and stressful situations, but with practice and dedication, we can develop the skill of being more patient. With patience, we can remain calm and collected in the face of life's challenges, and be better equipped to handle difficult people and situations. Patience can also give us the time to think things through and make better decisions, and allow us to be more understanding and compassionate towards others. Learning patience is a worthwhile endeavor that can help us to navigate life's difficulties more effectively.

Lastly, patience is an important life skill. It is the ability to remain calm and wait for the right moment to act instead of rushing into things. Patience can help us in many areas of our lives, from managing our emotions during difficult times to finding creative solutions to complex problems. It can also help us maintain healthy relationships and build strong bonds with those around us. Learning patience is essential for leading a successful and fulfilling life.

Trusting Yourself

Trust yourself and be confident in your abilities. Believe in yourself and your capabilities and don't let anyone tell you that you can't reach your goals. Taking risks and striving to achieve your goals can be difficult, but it can be one of the most rewarding experiences. Be true to yourself and your beliefs and don't let anyone else dictate your decisions. Trust that you are capable and that you can make a difference. Have faith in yourself and know that you can do anything you set your mind to.

Trusting yourself is an important part of life. It means having faith in your abilities and decisions, believing that you are capable of making the right choice for yourself. When you trust yourself, you are more likely to take risks and make bold decisions because you know they are right for you. This trust also helps you stay resilient in difficult times, as you know that you will be able to pull yourself through whatever comes your way. Trusting yourself is essential for living a fulfilled life and achieving your goals.

Self Discipline

Self-discipline is a powerful quality that empowers us to stay focused, motivated, and committed to our goals and aspirations. It is the ability to make conscious choices that align with our long-term vision, even when faced with distractions, temptations, or obstacles along the way. Self-discipline involves setting clear intentions and creating structured routines and habits that support our desired outcomes. It requires cultivating a strong sense of willpower, self-control, and the willingness to delay instant gratification for greater rewards in the future. By practicing self-discipline, we develop resilience, perseverance, and the capacity to overcome challenges and setbacks. It helps us build consistency, efficiency, and a strong work ethic in various areas of life. Self-discipline allows us to prioritize our time and energy effectively, making the most of each day and maximizing our potential. It empowers us to establish healthy boundaries, make responsible choices, and take ownership of our actions and decisions. Through self-discipline, we create a solid foundation for personal growth, success, and the realization of our full potential.

Self Discovery

Self-discovery is an extraordinary journey of exploration and introspection that unveils the depths of who we truly are. It involves delving into our inner world, uncovering our values, beliefs, strengths, and passions. It's about peeling back the layers of societal expectations, external influences, and conditioned patterns to reveal our authentic selves. Self-discovery is a process of self-reflection, asking meaningful questions, and listening to our intuition. It invites us to step outside our comfort zones, try new experiences, and embrace the unknown. Along this path, we may encounter challenges, face fears, and confront limiting beliefs, but these obstacles become opportunities for growth and transformation. Through self-discovery, we learn to cultivate self-acceptance, compassion, and love for ourselves. We gain clarity about our dreams, aspirations, and purpose, allowing us to align our lives with what truly matters to us. It is a lifelong journey that evolves with us, guiding us towards a sense of wholeness, fulfillment, and a deep connection to our authentic selves.

Self Worth

Discovering your self worth is an incredibly important part of life. It can be hard to understand and accept your own values, but it is essential to live a happy and fulfilled life. Taking the time to reflect on your strengths and weaknesses can help you to build a better understanding of yourself and your place in the world. When you recognize your self worth, you can learn to appreciate who you are and the unique gifts you have to offer. With this new found confidence, you can face life's challenges with optimism and courage, and find a new strength within yourself.

Spirituality

Getting in tune with your spirituality is a great way to gain a deeper understanding of yourself and the world around you. It can help you to become more mindful and present in the moment, allowing you to appreciate small moments and find the beauty in the world. Through connecting with your spirituality, you can find a sense of peace and connection to something greater than yourself. It can also help you to appreciate the simple things in life and become less materialistic. Connecting with your spirituality is an empowering and fulfilling experience that can have a positive effect on all aspects of your life.

Shadow Work

Shadow work is a process of exploring and healing the parts of ourselves that we may have unconsciously hidden away. It involves looking deeply into our unconscious parts, understanding our inner motivations and fears, and learning to accept our flaws and vulnerabilities. Shadow work can be a difficult and uncomfortable process, but it is an essential part of personal growth and self-awareness. Through this work, we can learn to embrace and accept all aspects of ourselves, and create a more balanced and healthy life.

Shadow work is an important process of self-exploration and healing that involves looking inward at our darker, hidden parts. It involves facing our inner demons, understanding our fears and traumas, and learning to accept and even love those parts of ourselves. Working on shadow work can be a difficult and uncomfortable process, but it is incredibly rewarding and can help us to live more authentically and in alignment with our values. It is a journey of self-discovery and growth, and can be a valuable tool for personal transformation.

Working on shadow work within yourself can be a challenging but incredibly rewarding process. It involves examining and uncovering the parts of yourself that you may not want to acknowledge or accept. It is a process of self-discovery and acceptance that can help you become more aware of who you are and how you operate in the world. Shadow work can help you confront your fears and challenges, learn to accept yourself, and ultimately, become a more confident and competent individual. It is an important task for personal growth and development, and it can open up new opportunities for growth and understanding.

Shadow work is the process of exploring the parts of yourself that you have kept hidden away, such as past experiences, repressed emotions, and unacknowledged patterns. It is a difficult but rewarding journey of self-discovery and healing that can help you to understand yourself better and to create more balance in your life. Working on shadow work within yourself is a process of identifying, understanding, and addressing the parts of yourself that you have kept hidden away. It is a process of recognizing the importance of the full range of your personality, and of reclaiming the parts of yourself that you have neglected or denied. Through this process, you can gain greater self-awareness, build resilience, and create more meaningful relationships.

Shadow work is an important part of personal development. It involves facing the parts of ourselves that we have been avoiding or ignoring, and bringing them into the light of awareness. This can involve examining our thoughts and feelings, allowing ourselves to be vulnerable and honest about our experiences, and confronting our fears and insecurities. Working on shadow work within ourselves can help us to become more authentic, and to gain insight into our motivations and patterns of behavior. It can also help us to understand ourselves better, and to create more meaningful relationships.

Positivity

Staying positive is an important life skill that will help you get through any challenge you may face. It's important to remember that no matter how tough life may seem, there is always something to be grateful for and something to look forward to. The key is to focus on the good and not get bogged down in the negative. Find things that can bring you joy, and actively engage in activities that make you feel good, like spending time with friends or family, taking a walk, or doing something creative. You can also practice positive self-talk, like reminding yourself of all the things you're good at and all the successes you've had in life. Finally, remember to be kind to yourself and to others, as this will help create a positive environment that will help you stay optimistic.

Learning Yourself

Learning yourself is an important and ongoing process. It involves taking the time to reflect on who you are, what you want out of life, and how you can best achieve it. Knowing yourself helps you to understand, accept, and appreciate your strengths and weaknesses. It also allows you to better manage yourself and your emotions, make better decisions, and build healthier relationships. Through learning yourself, you can become more self-aware and more confident in who you are and what you stand for. This can help you to lead a more fulfilled and meaningful life.

Peace With Yourself

Becoming at peace with yourself and life is a journey of self-discovery and understanding. It involves looking inward and gaining insight into who we are and why we feel the way we do. It is about accepting ourselves, our flaws, and our strengths, and using that understanding to craft a life that is meaningful and true. It is about being at ease in our own skin and having the courage to look honestly at our lives and make changes that will bring more peace and joy. It is a process of growth and empowerment that can lead to a life of greater contentment and satisfaction.

Avoid Negativity

In order to keep negativity out of your life, it is important to focus on the good things that are happening and to try to stay away from people and situations that bring you down. It is easy to get caught up in the negative aspects of life, but it is important to remain positive and to take time out of each day to do something that brings you joy. The more positive you remain, the less likely it is that negative thoughts will take over your life. Additionally, it is important to surround yourself with positive people and to be mindful of how your thoughts, words, and actions can affect those around you. Keeping negativity out of your life can be a difficult task, but it is worth the effort.

Avoid Repeating Past Mistakes

To avoid repeating past mistakes, it is important to reflect and learn from previous experiences. Firstly, one must take the time to acknowledge past mistakes and understand the reasons behind them. This can involve evaluating one's decisions, thought processes, and any negative patterns that contributed to the mistake. Next, it is crucial to develop self-awareness and identify red flags that may lead to similar errors in the future. This could include recognizing recurring negative emotions or circumstances that pave the way for poor choices. Once identified, it is wise to actively work on developing alternative strategies or approaches to avoid falling into the same traps. Seeking guidance from insightful mentors or professionals can also provide valuable perspectives to navigate complex situations. Finally, it is essential to practice mindfulness and reflection regularly, allowing for constant self-improvement and growth. By consciously applying these measures, individuals can break the cycle of repeated mistakes and pave the way for future success.

Understanding

Learning to be understanding is a transformative journey that requires an open heart and a willingness to see the world through different lenses. It starts with cultivating empathy, the ability to truly connect with others and understand their emotions and experiences. Actively listening, without judgment or interruption, allows us to create a safe space for others to share their thoughts and feelings. Being open-minded is crucial, as it enables us to challenge our own biases and preconceptions, and embrace the diversity of perspectives that exist in the world. Patience is a virtue that allows us to give others the time and space they need to express themselves fully. Seeking knowledge about different cultures, beliefs, and experiences expands our understanding and broadens our horizons. Self-reflection is a vital component of this process, as it helps us examine our own thoughts, feelings, and actions, and make necessary adjustments to enhance our understanding. Ultimately, learning to be understanding is a lifelong journey of growth and compassion, where we strive to create a more empathetic and harmonious world.

The Unconscious Mind

Learning about your unconscious mind can be a fascinating and enlightening journey. The unconscious mind refers to the vast reservoir of thoughts, feelings, and memories that are not readily accessible to our conscious awareness. It is like a hidden part of our psyche that influences our thoughts, emotions, and behaviors in ways we may not even be aware of.

Exploring the unconscious mind can help us gain a deeper understanding of ourselves, our motivations, and our patterns of behavior. It can reveal hidden fears, desires, and beliefs that may be holding us back or influencing our decisions without our conscious knowledge. By bringing these unconscious processes into awareness, we can begin to work through them, overcome any limitations they may impose, and experience personal growth and transformation.

There are various techniques and approaches to uncover and explore the unconscious mind. Psychoanalysis, dream analysis, hypnosis, and mindfulness practices are just a few examples. These different methods can help us tap into the deeper layers of our consciousness and uncover hidden aspects of ourselves.

Self Control

Having self-control is a valuable skill that enables us to regulate our thoughts, emotions, and behaviors in order to make deliberate, conscious choices. It involves being aware of our impulses and desires while exerting restraint and discipline. With self-control, we can resist immediate gratification and make decisions that align with our long-term goals and values. It allows us to manage stress, handle conflicts, and navigate challenging situations with composure and rationality. Self-control empowers us to overcome bad habits, break destructive patterns, and cultivate healthier behaviors. It helps us stay focused and maintain productivity, even when faced with distractions or temptations. By exercising self-control, we enhance our decision-making abilities and build a solid foundation for personal growth and success. It is a skill that can be honed through practice, mindfulness, and self-awareness. Ultimately, having self-control allows us to lead more balanced, purposeful lives and make choices that contribute to our overall well-being and fulfillment.

Grief

Dealing with grief is a deeply personal and challenging process, and there's no one-size-fits-all approach. However, there are some strategies that may help you navigate through this difficult time. Firstly, it's important to allow yourself to feel and express your emotions. Recognize that grief is a natural response to loss and give yourself permission to experience a range of emotions, including sadness, anger, and confusion. Seek support from others, whether it's through talking to friends, family, or joining a support group, as connecting with others who have experienced similar loss can provide comfort and understanding. Taking care of your physical and mental health is crucial. Engage in self-care activities like exercise, getting enough rest, and maintaining a healthy routine. Be patient and kind to yourself as you heal, understanding that the grieving process takes time and there is no set timeline for recovery. If you find that your grief becomes overwhelming or significantly impacts your daily life, consider seeking professional help from a therapist or counselor who specializes in grief counseling. Remember, everyone's grief journey is unique, so be gentle with yourself and allow yourself to heal in your own way.

Being Whole

Being whole for yourself is about cultivating a sense of inner fulfillment and well-being that doesn't rely solely on external factors or validation from others. It means recognizing your worth and embracing your individuality. Start by practicing self-acceptance and self-compassion. Treat yourself with kindness and understanding, honoring your strengths and acknowledging your imperfections without judgment. Nurture your physical, mental, and emotional well-being by engaging in activities that bring you joy, practicing self-care, and setting boundaries to protect your energy and prioritize your needs. Cultivate a positive mindset by focusing on gratitude, affirmations, and fostering a growth mindset that allows you to learn and grow from life's challenges. Engage in activities that help you discover and develop your passions, talents, and interests. Surround yourself with supportive and uplifting people who inspire and encourage you. Remember, being whole for yourself is an ongoing journey of self-discovery and self-love. It's about valuing and prioritizing your own happiness and well-being, ultimately creating a fulfilling and balanced life that aligns with your authentic self.

Wanting To Live

Wanting to live is a powerful affirmation of the value and potential that life holds. It is a testament to the resilience and strength within us. When we embrace the desire to live, we open ourselves up to the possibilities that each day brings. It means finding meaning and purpose in our existence, pursuing our passions, and building connections with others. Wanting to live is about cherishing the beauty of life's simple moments, finding joy in the little things, and appreciating the wonders of the world around us. It involves setting goals, striving for personal growth, and embracing the journey of self-discovery. It also means reaching out for support when needed, seeking help in times of difficulty, and finding solace in the presence of loved ones. Wanting to live is a testament to our resilience, our ability to overcome challenges, and our determination to make the most of the time we have. It is a reminder that life is a precious gift, and every day holds the potential for growth, connection, and endless possibilities.

Personal Development

Personal development is an ongoing process of self-improvement and growth. It involves setting goals, acquiring new knowledge and skills, and developing self-awareness. The journey of personal development is unique to each individual, as it is driven by their passions, values, and aspirations. It requires dedication, perseverance, and a willingness to step outside of one's comfort zone.

One of the key aspects of personal development is setting goals. Goals provide a sense of direction and purpose, and they serve as a roadmap for personal growth. By setting clear, achievable goals, individuals can stay focused on their desired outcomes and work towards them with determination.

Another important aspect of personal development is acquiring new knowledge and skills. This could be through formal education, taking up new hobbies, or seeking out experiences that challenge and expand one's abilities. Continuous learning and development not only enhance personal growth but also open up new opportunities and perspectives.

Self-awareness is a fundamental component of personal development. It involves understanding one's strengths and weaknesses

Suicide Awareness

Suicide awareness is an important issue that continues to gain attention and recognition in society today. It involves understanding the factors that contribute to suicidal thoughts, recognizing warning signs, and providing support to those who may be struggling. Advocacy and education surrounding suicide awareness aim to break the stigma surrounding mental health and promote open conversations about emotional well-being. By raising awareness about the resources available, such as helplines, counseling services, and mental health professionals, we can all play a role in preventing suicide and offering hope and understanding to those who need it most. It is essential to remember that everyone's experiences and struggles are unique, and lending a non-judgmental ear or offering a helping hand can make all the difference in someone's journey towards healing and recovery.

Affirmations

I'M IMPORTANT
I'M STRONG
I'M LOVED
I'M PATIENT
I'M KIND
I'M HUMBLE
I'M NOT DEFINED BY MY PAST
I'M AN AMAZING PERSON
I'M PERFECT THE WAY I AM
I'M UNDERSTANDING
I'M WORTHY
I'M BEAUTIFUL INSIDE AND OUT
I'M EVOLVING
I'M ME

Embracing Imperfections

In a world that often glorifies perfection, it is crucial to recognize that being imperfect does not diminish one's worth or strength. Society's unrealistic expectations and the constant pursuit of flawlessness can lead individuals to doubt themselves and their abilities. However, it is essential to understand that imperfections are what make us unique and human. This essay explores the idea that despite our imperfections, we are still worthy and possess an inner strength that enables us to overcome challenges and thrive.

The Essence of Individuality. Imperfections are not flaws to be ashamed of; they are the very essence of our individuality. Each person possesses a unique set of imperfections that shape their character and contribute to their personal growth. These imperfections allow us to learn from our mistakes, develop resilience, and foster empathy towards others. Embracing our imperfections enables us to accept ourselves wholly and appreciate the beauty of our uniqueness.

Beyond Perfection. Perfection is an unattainable standard that society often imposes on individuals. However, worthiness is not contingent upon achieving perfection. Our worth is inherent and should not be determined by external factors or societal expectations. Recognizing our worthiness allows us to cultivate self-love, confidence, and a positive self-image. It is through embracing our imperfections that we can truly appreciate our inherent worth and value as individuals.

Nurturing Resilience. Strength is not solely derived from physical prowess or the absence of flaws. True strength lies within our ability to face adversity, overcome challenges, and grow from our experiences. Imperfections provide us with opportunities to develop resilience, determination, and perseverance. It is through acknowledging and accepting our imperfections that we can tap into our inner strength and harness it to navigate life's obstacles.

Growth and Self-Improvement. Imperfections should not be viewed as limitations but rather as catalysts for growth and self-improvement. By acknowledging our imperfections, we open ourselves up to personal development and self-reflection. Embracing our flaws allows us to identify areas for improvement and work towards becoming the best versions of ourselves. It is through this process that we can continuously evolve and grow, both personally and professionally.

Empathy and Connection. Our imperfections not only shape our own journey but also allow us to connect with others on a deeper level. By embracing our flaws, we create an environment of empathy and understanding, fostering genuine connections with those around us. Sharing our vulnerabilities and imperfections can inspire others to embrace their own uniqueness and find strength in their perceived weaknesses. Through our authenticity, we can empower others to recognize their worth and inner strength.

In Conclusion, In a world fixated on perfection, it is crucial to remember that imperfections do not diminish our worth or strength. Embracing our flaws allows us to appreciate our individuality, nurture our inner strength, and foster personal growth. By acknowledging our imperfections, we can inspire others to embrace their own uniqueness and find strength in their perceived weaknesses. Let us celebrate our imperfections, for they are the very qualities that make us worthy and strong.

You Are Enough

In a society that often measures worth based on external achievements and comparisons, it is essential to recognize that we are more than enough just as we are. The constant pressure to prove ourselves and meet unrealistic standards can lead to feelings of inadequacy and self-doubt. However, it is crucial to understand that our value extends far beyond societal expectations. This essay explores the idea that we are inherently more than enough, possessing unique qualities and potential that make us valuable individuals.

Beyond External Validation. Our worth is not determined by external validation or the opinions of others. Each individual possesses inherent value simply by existing. Our worth is not contingent upon achievements, possessions, or societal standards. Recognizing our inherent value allows us to embrace our true selves and appreciate the unique qualities that make us who we are.

Unveiling Our True Potential. Being more than enough means embracing our authenticity and recognizing the power of our true potential. When we let go of the need to conform or compare ourselves to others, we unlock the ability to tap into our unique talents, passions, and strengths. Embracing our authentic selves allows us to discover and pursue our true purpose, leading to a fulfilling and meaningful life.

Embracing Imperfections. Self-acceptance is a vital aspect of recognizing that we are more than enough. It involves embracing our imperfections and understanding that they do not diminish our value. Imperfections are what make us human and provide opportunities for growth and self-improvement. By accepting and embracing our flaws, we can cultivate self-love and compassion, allowing us to fully appreciate our worthiness.

The Journey of Growth. Being more than enough does not mean being perfect; it means acknowledging our progress and growth. Life is a continuous journey of learning and evolving. By celebrating our achievements, no matter how small, we recognize our capacity for growth and development. Each step forward, each lesson learned, contributes to our overall growth and reinforces our belief in our inherent value.

Sharing Our Gifts. Recognizing our inherent value and embracing our potential allows us to make a positive impact on others. By sharing our unique gifts, talents, and perspectives, we inspire and uplift those around us. Our contributions, no matter how small, can create a ripple effect of positivity and change. Being more than enough means recognizing the power we have to make a difference in the lives of others.

In Conclusion, In a world that often emphasizes external achievements and comparisons, it is crucial to remember that we are more than enough just as we are. Our inherent value extends beyond societal expectations and external validation. Embracing our authenticity, accepting our imperfections, and celebrating our progress allows us to recognize our true potential. By embracing our worthiness and sharing our unique gifts, we can make a positive impact on the world around us. Let us embrace the truth that we are more than enough and live our lives with confidence, purpose, and a deep appreciation for our inherent value.

Proud To Be Alive

Being alive is a remarkable gift that we often take for granted. In a world filled with challenges, uncertainties, and hardships, it is essential to recognize and be proud of the mere fact that we are alive. Life itself is a precious opportunity, and embracing it with gratitude and pride can transform our perspective and enrich our experiences.

Every day, we wake up to a world full of possibilities, where we have the chance to create, learn, grow, and connect with others. The very act of being alive grants us the ability to experience a wide range of emotions, to pursue our dreams, and to make a positive impact on the lives of those around us.

Being proud of being alive means acknowledging the resilience and strength it takes to navigate the ups and downs of life. It means recognizing the inherent value and potential within ourselves and embracing the unique journey we are on. Each of us has overcome obstacles, faced adversity, and triumphed in our own ways. Being proud of being alive is a testament to our ability to persevere and find joy even in the face of adversity.

Moreover, being proud of being alive allows us to appreciate the beauty and wonder that surrounds us. From the breathtaking landscapes to the intricate complexities of human relationships, life offers us countless opportunities for awe and inspiration. By embracing our existence with pride, we open ourselves up to fully experiencing and savoring the richness of life.

Being proud of being alive also means recognizing the interconnectedness of all living beings. We are part of a vast web of life, and our presence has an impact on the world around us. By being proud of our existence, we can cultivate a sense of responsibility and purpose, striving to make a positive difference in the lives of others and in the world as a whole.

In conclusion, being proud of being alive is a powerful affirmation of our gratitude, resilience, and potential. It is a recognition of the preciousness of life and a commitment to embracing its challenges and joys. Let us celebrate the gift of life, be proud of our existence, and strive to make the most of every moment we are given.

Keep Trying

In the face of obstacles, setbacks, and failures, the act of keep trying holds immense power. It is a testament to our resilience, determination, and unwavering belief in our abilities. Keep trying is not just a mere action; it is a mindset that propels us forward, fuels our growth, and leads us towards success.

Life is filled with challenges and uncertainties, and it is easy to become discouraged or disheartened when faced with obstacles. However, keep trying reminds us that failure is not the end but rather an opportunity for growth and learning. It is through perseverance and the willingness to keep trying that we can overcome adversity and achieve our goals.

Keep trying is a reflection of our belief in ourselves and our dreams. It is a refusal to give up, even when the odds seem insurmountable. By persisting in the face of difficulties, we demonstrate our commitment to our aspirations and our unwavering belief that we are capable of achieving them.

Moreover, keep trying allows us to discover our true potential. It pushes us beyond our comfort zones, encouraging us to explore new possibilities and embrace growth. Each attempt, even if it ends in failure, provides valuable lessons and insights that contribute to our personal and professional development.

Keep trying also inspires others. Our determination and resilience can serve as a source of motivation and encouragement for those around us. By demonstrating our commitment to keep trying, we show others that setbacks are not permanent roadblocks but temporary detours on the path to success.

In the grand tapestry of life, keep trying is the thread that weaves together our dreams, aspirations, and achievements. It is the driving force that propels us forward, even when the journey becomes arduous. It is a reminder that success is not solely defined by the absence of failure but by the willingness to persevere and keep trying despite it.

In conclusion, keep trying is a powerful mindset that fuels our growth, resilience, and success. It is a reflection of our unwavering belief in ourselves and our dreams. By embracing the power of keep trying, we can overcome obstacles, discover our true potential, and inspire others along the way. Let us embrace the mindset of keep trying and continue to strive towards our goals, knowing that our efforts will ultimately lead us to success.

Thank You, For Choosing To Live!